Robyn Pandolph

Needleturn Appliqué
MADE EASY

LANDAUER BOOKS

Robyn Pandolph

NEEDLETURN APPLIQUÉ
MADE EASY

Quilt Design Copyright © 2004 By Robyn Pandolph

Copyright © 2004 By Landauer Corporation

This book was designed and produced by Landauer Books
A division of Landauer Corporation
12251 Maffitt Road, Cumming, Iowa 50061

President and Publisher: Jeramy Lanigan Landauer
Editor-in-Chief: Becky Johnston
Project Editor: Jill Reber
Art Director: Linda L. Bender
Project Designer: Margaret Sindelar
Technical Assistance: Patty Barrett
Photographers: Craig Anderson, Dennis Kennedy

Printed in USA.

Library of Congress Cataloging-in-Publication Data available on request.

ISBN: 1-890621-69-2

10 9 8 7 6 5 4 3 2 1

Introduction

What is needleturn appliqué? Simply stated, it is a form of hand appliqué in which the needle is used as a tool to turn the seam allowance under the appliqué before stitching it to the background using tiny stitches. Robyn Pandolph shares her secrets for needleturn appliqué made easy by offering her unique glue-basting technique and several alternate methods for applying the fabric pieces to the background. Whether you choose Robyn's freezer-paper-with-glue basting, freezer-paper-with-pin basting, or template plastic-with-thread basting, you'll learn the same simple techniques for making needleturn appliqué your favorite pastime. Starting with Robyn's stylized folk art heart, you can quickly learn the basics of needleturn and be ready to move on to the practice projects.

Throughout her many years of teaching, Robyn has often used her six-block quilt *My Favorite Things* as a terrific tool for learning needleturn appliqué. From the six blocks which range from the simple heart to the more challenging bee skep featuring the bias bar technique, beginners can master the challenges of everything from outer and inner curves and corners to narrow points and reverse appliqué.

Once the blocks are completed and the quilt is assembled, use the practice projects to complement the quilt for a glorious bed, bath or gift collection inspired by Robyn Pandolph's enduring folk art designs. Fabrics used throughout are from the *Sentimental Journey* collection Robyn designed for South Sea Imports®.

Table of Contents

8

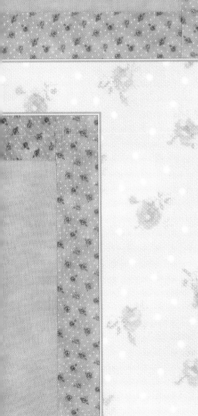

The Techniques

with Step-by Step Instructions
for My Favorite Things

From the six blocks featured here you can master the challenges of needleturn—everything from outer and inner curves and corners to narrow points, bias bars, and reverse appliqué. The step-by-step instructions make it easy to visualize and follow each needleturn appliqué technique.

As a traditional form of hand appliqué, the needle is used as a tool to turn the seam allowance under the appliqué before stitching it to the background using tiny stitches. Thus, the name needleturn appliqué. On the following pages you'll find Robyn's unique freezer-paper with-glue basting method. Use it for applying the fabric pieces to the background or choose from several alternate methods. Using Robyn's method (which eliminates the need for pin or thread basting), you'll learn a quick and easy technique for making needleturn appliqué your favorite portable pastime. By working one block at a time, after the appliqué pieces are cut and applied to the background square you can take it with you almost anywhere to practice the art of needleturn appliqué.

Starting with Robyn's stylized folk art heart, you can quickly learn the basic techniques of needleturn appliqué. After completing the six blocks for the My Favorite Things quilt, you'll have mastered the challenges and be ready to move on to the practice projects.

Supplies

for NEEDLETURN APPLIQUÉ

Scissors for cutting fabric

Scissors for cutting paper

Rotary cutter, mat and ruler

Freezer paper

Template plastic

Sandpaper or sandpaper board

Sewing marker fine point wash out or fade out

Permanent marker fine point

Needles: size 10; straw, sharps or milliners *or* your size
    and preference

Basting Glue (Roxanne's Glue-Baste-It™)

Silk pins and/or appliqué pins

Glue stick

Bias bars

Iron

Thimble (optional)

FABRIC YARDAGES WILL BE LISTED UNDER EACH PROJECT

Robyn Pandolph's Unique Technique
Glue Basting
Freezer Paper Templates

On the following pages you'll find Robyn's unique freezer-paper-with-glue basting method. Use it for applying the fabric pieces to the background or choose from several alternate methods. Using Robyn's method which eliminates the need for pin or thread basting, you'll learn a quick and easy technique for making needleturn appliqué your favorite portable pastime.

By working one block at a time, after the appliqué pieces are cut and applied to the background square you can take it with you almost anywhere to practice the art of needleturn appliqué.

After learning Robyn's method for using freezer paper templates with glue basting, you might want to review the two alternate methods which could prove useful in limited applications.

Whether you choose Robyn's unique method or a combination of all three techniques, the results are sure to ensure success in your pursuit of perfection in needleturn appliqué.

Refer to the step-by-step instructions on the following pages using the heart design from Block 3 (page 48). This simple shape allows for a complete lesson in mastering the challenges of needleturn appliqué.

1 Trace design using pencil or fine point permanent marker onto paper side (dull) of freezer paper. Number the pieces, if the block has many motifs.

2 Cut out freezer paper template on traced line using paper scissors. It is helpful to store all the pieces for one block in a plastic bag.

3 Place freezer paper template waxed (shiny) side down to the right side of desired fabric. At this time be sure to position the fabric design, if desired. Leave about ½" between pieces. Press using a dry iron, cotton setting.

4 Draw around freezer paper template using an ultra fine tip permanent marker. Be sure to protect your table surface.

Glue Basting
FREEZER PAPER TEMPLATES

5 Cut out appliqué piece using fabric scissors. Leave a narrow width of fabric extending ⅛" to ¼" beyond the traced line.

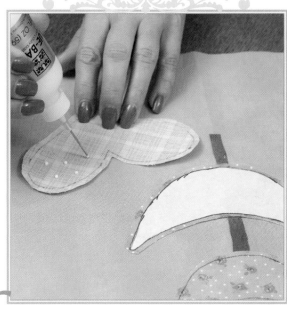

6 Lay out the appliqué pieces working from the back of the design forward. Glue using small dots of Roxanne's Glue Baste-It™. Glue should be far enough away from the drawn line for the seam allowance to fold in. Remove freezer paper templates after you glue baste.

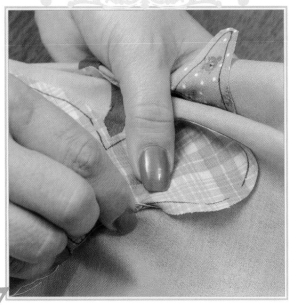

7a Thread a needle with thread to match the appliqué piece. Holding the fabric between thumb and forefinger and using your needle as a tool, fold under the seam allowance. Appliqué slip stitch to the background fabric, making sure to turn under the entire black line.

7b To make an appliqué slip stitch, begin by working on the front of your block. Using your needle as a tool, fold under the seam allowance. Bring needle up from the background catching a few threads of the appliqué piece at the fold.
   Go back into the background where the needle was brought out. Try to keep stitches ⅛" or smaller. Repeat.

Glue Basting
FREEZER PAPER TEMPLATES

8 Working on an INSIDE CURVE, and using sharp scissors, clip just through the black line. The tighter the curve the more you will need to clip. If you do not clip through the black line it will be difficult to turn the line all the way under.

9 Working on an OUTSIDE CURVE, trim the seam allowance closer to the black line to reduce bulk. You do not need to clip an OUTSIDE CURVE. Use you thumb to ease in fullness. Make sure stitches are close together.

10a Working on an INSIDE CORNER, and using sharp scissors, clip just through the black line. If you do not clip through the black line it will be difficult to turn the line all the way under. Continue to appliqué slip stitch to the inside corner. Take an extra stitch on this side of the corner.

10b To help with this corner, place a dot of Roxanne's Glue Baste-It™ on a piece of paper. Place the tip of the needle in the glue. This little bit of glue will help with tucking in stray threads. Tuck in the other side and continue appliqué slip stitching.

Glue Basting
FREEZER PAPER TEMPLATES

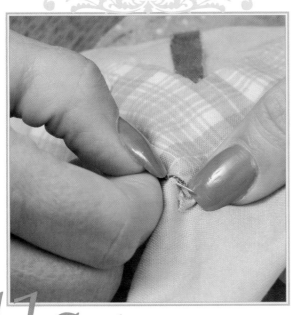

11a Working on an OUTSIDE CORNER OR OUTSIDE POINT, slip stitch to within ⅛" to ¼" of the corner. Take your last stitch in the background only.

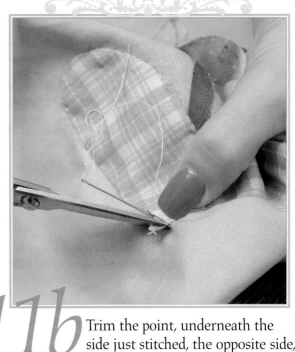

11b Trim the point, underneath the side just stitched, the opposite side, and the tip.

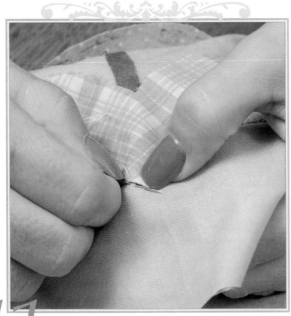

11c Turn the point under to where the last stitch was taken. Grab the point with the needle and finish the stitch. Take one more whole stitch on the point. Needleturn the other side and continue stitching.

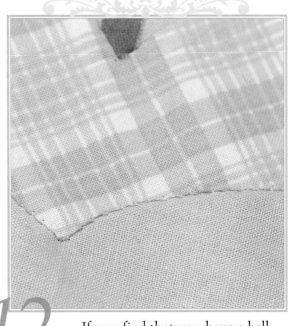

12 If you find that you have a ball on the end of the fabric point, then next time trim a little more in advance. This takes practice. Remember this is folk art and does not need to be perfect. To press your finished block follow instructions on page 23.

Glue Basting
FREEZER PAPER TEMPLATES

ALTERNATE TECHNIQUE
Pin Basting
FREEZER PAPER TEMPLATES

In this alternate needleturn appliqué technique, the freezer paper template serves as a foundation for the fabric shape to be appliquéd as you use the needle to turn the edge of the fabric under and stitch it to the background. For a single appliqué shape, freezer paper is durable enough to use for needleturn. However, even though you can re-press the freezer paper a few times, it is best to use template plastic for multiple appliqué shapes (see page 24). The freezer paper method will also prove helpful when the shape is rather large (such as the bee skep), as the freezer paper helps to stabilize the fabric of the appliqué shape.

Freezer paper is inexpensive and can be purchased in most supermarkets where aluminum foil and waxed paper are sold. Freezer paper has two distinct sides. The paper side is dull. The waxed or light plastic side is shiny. Make sure the dull paper side is face up for tracing. The waxed shiny side will stick to the right side of the fabric when pressed with an iron, but is easily removed after pressing.

With the freezer paper method, pattern pieces do not need to be reversed. Trace patterns exactly the size and direction as shown. A seam allowance will be added to the fabric shape later, before it is cut out.

Refer to the step-by-step instructions on the following pages using the heart design from Block 3 (page 48). This simple shape allows for a complete lesson in mastering the challenges of needleturn appliqué.

19

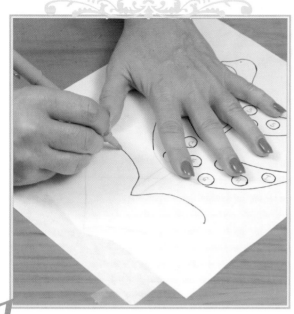

1 Trace design using pencil or fine point permanent marker onto paper side (dull) of freezer paper. Number the pieces, if the block has many motifs.

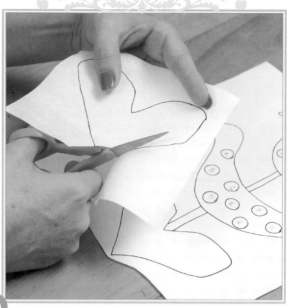

2 Cut out freezer paper shape on traced line using paper scissors. It is helpful to store all the pieces for one block in a plastic bag.

3 Place freezer paper template waxed (shiny) side down to the right side of desired fabric. At this time be sure to position the fabric design, if desired. Leave about ½" between pieces. Press using a dry iron, cotton setting.

4 Draw around freezer paper template using an ultra fine tip permanent marker. Be sure to protect your table surface.

Pin Basting
FREEZER PAPER TEMPLATES

5 Cut out appliqué piece, using fabric scissors. Leave a narrow width of fabric extending ⅛" to ¼" beyond the traced line.

6 Lay out the appliqué pieces working from the back of the design forward. Using silk pins or appliqué pins, pin piece to desired location on the background fabric.

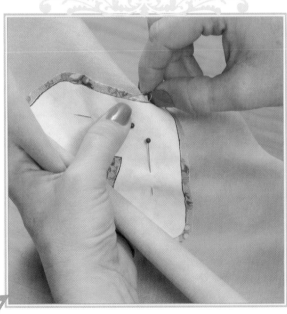

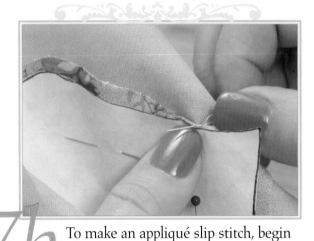

7a Thread a needle with thread to match the appliqué piece. Holding the fabric between thumb and forefinger and using your needle as a tool, fold under the seam allowance. Appliqué slip stitch to the background fabric.

7b To make an appliqué slip stitch, begin by working on the front of your block. Using your needle as a tool, fold under the seam allowance. Bring needle up from the background catching a few threads of the appliqué piece at the fold.
Go back into the background where the needle was brought out. Try to keep stitches ⅛" or smaller. Repeat.

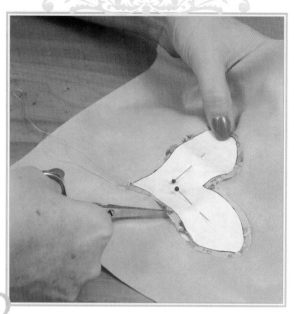

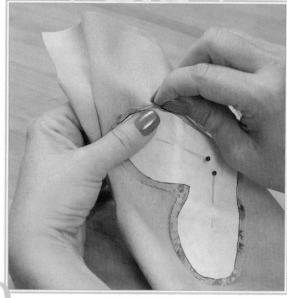

8 Working on an INSIDE CURVE and using the points of sharp scissors, clip to within a few threads of traced line. Clip as needed to get the smooth fold at edge. Use needle to turn fabric and slip stitch.

9 Working on an OUTSIDE CURVE, trim the seam allowance closer to the traced line to reduce bulk. You do not need to clip an outer curve. Use your thumb to hold the fabric in place and your needle to ease in the fullness. Make sure stitches are close together.

10a

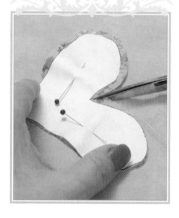

Working on an INSIDE CORNER, and using sharp scissors, clip to within a few threads of the traced line.
Continue to slip stitch to center of corner. Take an extra stitch on each side of corner to secure.

10b

Working on an INSIDE CORNER, run your needle through a glue stick. Picking up a bit of glue will help hold the frayed ends in place while you slip stitch.

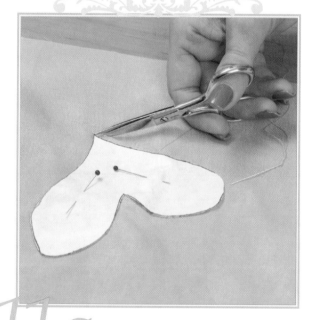

11a Working on an OUTSIDE CORNER or point, clip the corner square to the shape.

Pin Basting
FREEZER PAPER TEMPLATES

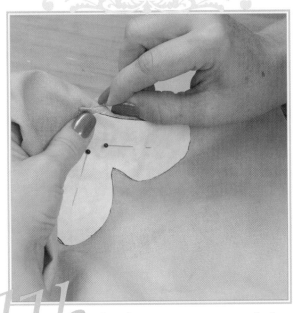

11b Clip the corner square to help remove the bulk out of the seam allowance. Take an extra stitch at the point to secure.

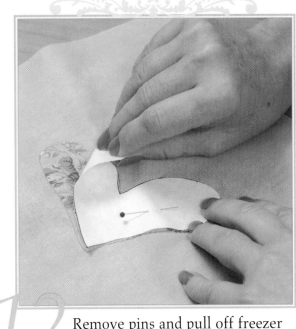

12 Remove pins and pull off freezer paper.

13 Press appliqué, placing the block face down on a padded surface. A terry towel works well.

14 Admire your finished block!

ALTERNATE TECHNIQUE
Thread Basting
TEMPLATE PLASTIC

For making one or more appliqué shapes, it is best to use template plastic. Because a firm plastic template can be used repeatedly, it is only necessary to trace the design from the pattern once.

Choose a template plastic that is not too stiff and can be easily cut with paper scissors. Be sure that your template has a smooth edge, especially on curves.

Refer to the step-by-step instructions on the following pages using the heart design from Block 3 (page 48). This simple shape allows for a complete lesson in mastering the challenges of needleturn appliqué.

1 Trace design onto template plastic using a fine tip permanent marker.

2 Cut out plastic template on the traced line using paper scissors. It is helpful to store all the pieces for one block in a plastic bag.

3 Work on a piece of sandpaper or a sandpaper board to prevent the fabric from slipping. At this time be sure to position the fabric's design such as the rose, above, in a pleasing arrangement. Draw around template using a fine tipped fabric marker.

4a Cut out appliqué piece, using fabric scissors. Leave a narrow width of fabric extending ⅛" to ¼" beyond the traced line.

4b Begin cutting at base of heart as shown here.

Thread Basting
TEMPLATE PLASTIC

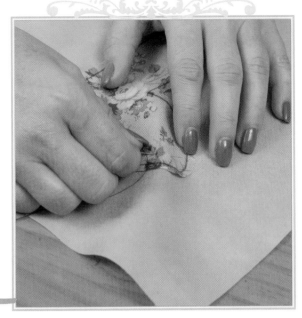

5 Position appliqué piece in desired location on the background fabric and thread baste to hold.

6a Thread a needle with thread to match the appliqué piece. Holding the fabric between thumb and forefinger and using your needle as a tool, fold under the seam allowance. Appliqué slip stitch to the background fabric.

6b To make an appliqué slip stitch, begin by working on the front of your block.
    Using your needle as a tool, fold under the seam allowance. Bring needle up from the background catching a few threads of the appliqué piece at the fold. Go back into the background where the needle was brought out. Try to keep stitches ⅛" or smaller. Repeat.

7 Working on an INSIDE CURVE, clip using the points of sharp scissors to within a few threads of traced line. Clip as needed to get the smooth fold at edge. Use needle to turn fabric and slip stitch.

Thread Basting
TEMPLATE PLASTIC

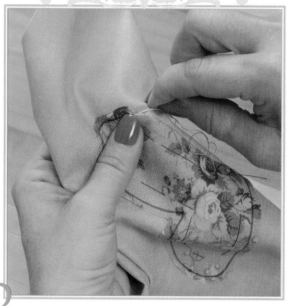

8 Working on an OUTSIDE CURVE, trim the seam allowance close to the traced line to reduce bulk. There is no need to clip an outer curve. Use the needle to ease in the fullness. Your thumb will help hold fabric in place. Make sure stitches are close together.

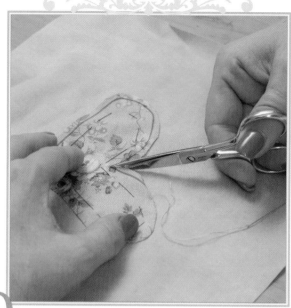

9a Working on an INSIDE CORNER and using sharp scissors, clip to within a few threads of the traced line. Continue to slip stitch to center of corner. Take an extra stitch on each side of corner to secure.

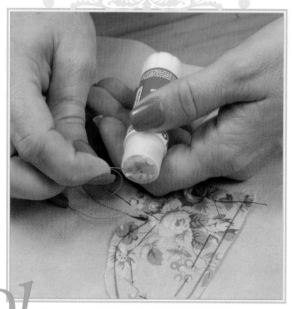

9b Working on an INSIDE CORNER, run your needle through a glue stick. Picking up a bit of glue will help hold the frayed ends in place while you slip stitch.

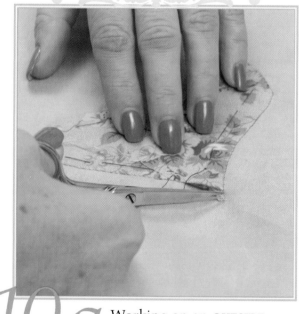

10a Working on an OUTSIDE CORNER or point, clip the corner square to the shape. This will help remove the bulk out of the seam allowance.

Thread Basting
TEMPLATE PLASTIC

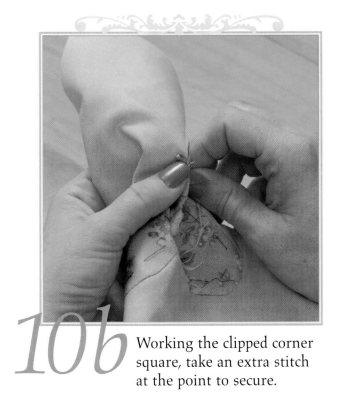

10b Working the clipped corner square, take an extra stitch at the point to secure.

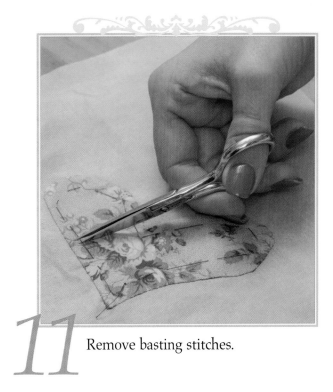

11 Remove basting stitches.

12 Press appliqué, placing the block face down on a padded surface. A terry towel will work best.

13 Admire your finished block!

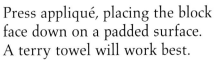

Thread Basting
TEMPLATE PLASTIC

ADDITIONAL TECHNIQUE
Reverse Appliqué

The reverse appliqué technique is a simple method of cutting out a portion of the appliqué shape so that after it is applied, a portion of the background fabric shows through the opening. The leaf for the flower featured on Block 5 offers the perfect opportunity to practice reverse appliqué.

However, to better demonstrate this technique, an enlarged leaf pattern is suggested for practicing reverse appliqué. Using the pattern on page 33, trace the leaf onto freezer paper or template plastic. Trace the middle opening of the leaf. Trace around leaf onto the right side of fabric. Trace the center opening, as well. Refer to the step-by-step instructions on the following pages using the enlarged leaf pattern. This simple shape allows for a complete lesson in mastering the challenges of reverse appliqué.

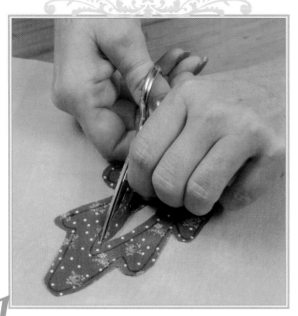

1 Refer to Steps 1–4a (page 26) to prepare shape for appliqué. Cut out opening in center of leaf for reverse appliqué leaving a ⅛" seam allowance.

2 Position appliqué piece in desired location on the background fabric and baste to hold. Or, use baste-it glue (Robyn uses Roxanne's Baste-It™) and following manufacturer's directions, lift edges of appliqué and add a few drops of glue to secure.

3 Clip curves and corners to within a few threads of traced line.

4 Starting at center opening appliqué slip stitch the curve using thread to match the appliqué piece. Remove basting stitches.

Reverse Appliqué

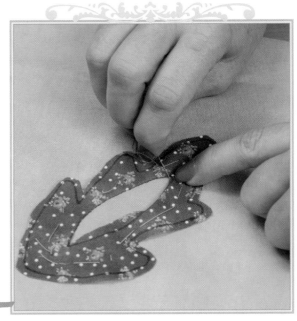

5 Stitch the inside corner of center opening. A bit of glue stick on your needle may prove to be helpful. Finish the leaf appliqué by slip stitching outside of leaf.

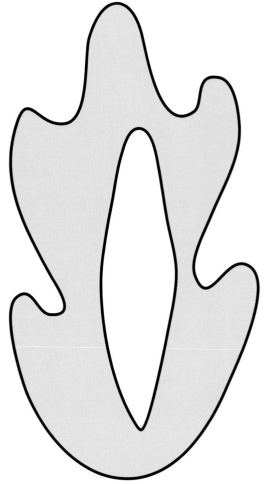

Use this enlarged pattern for practice only. The leaf is larger than the pattern for the flower appliqué for Block 5 shown on page 52.

Reverse Appliqué

ADDITIONAL TECHNIQUE
Bias Bar

Fabric cut on the bias and sewn into strips will more easily bend and curve into the desired shape for your design.

Refer to the step-by-step instructions on the following pages to cut fabric on the bias for a 12" x 44" strip for the bee skep design from Block 6 (page 54). This bias bar technique allows for a complete lesson in mastering the challenges of needleturn appliqué.

Cutting a bias strip

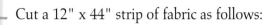

1

Cut strips width indicated in pattern following these instructions using a rotary cutter, mat and ruler.

Cut a 12" x 44" strip of fabric as follows:

a

Lay one layer of fabric right side up, on cutting mat. Align ruler at 45º angle to long edge, as shown below.

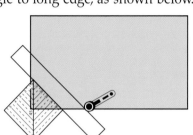

b

From this clean edge measure and cut strips the width indicated in pattern. For practice, 1¼" works well.

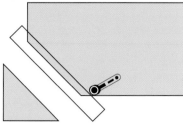

c

To join strips stitch as shown to length needed. Sew, right sides together, using ¼" seam allowance.

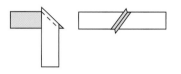

2

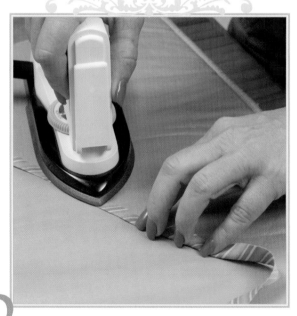

Press the bias strip in half horizontally being careful to not stretch the fabric.

3

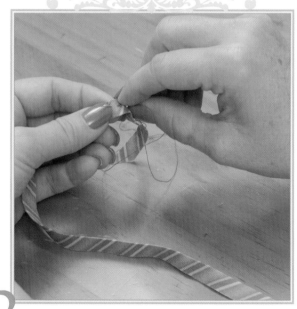

Machine-stitch the seam allowance using a smaller stitch length (2/2.5) as close as possible to the edge so that when the seam is trimmed the stitching holds. Or, hand baste a seam allowance.

Note: Choose appropriate size bias bar to make sure it will easily slip inside the bias fabric tube.

Bias Bar

4 Insert appropriate size bias bar into the bias fabric tube.

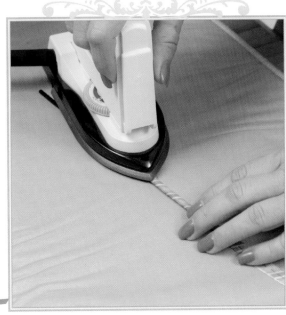

5 Press on top side of strip (with bias bar inside) rolling the seam allowance to the back (under side). Keep moving the bias bar along as needed.

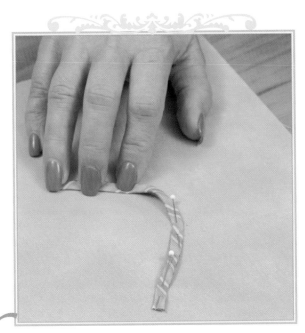

6 Pin or glue the completed bias strip onto your design, turning and curving it as indicated on the pattern. Appliqué slip stitch in place. Make sure to tuck in seam allowance at end of bias strip.

Bias Bar

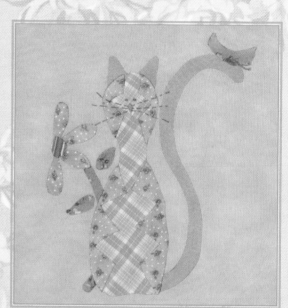

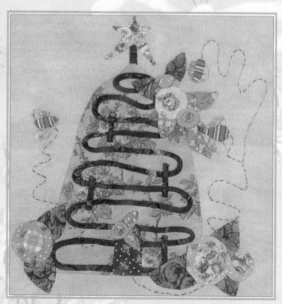

The Blocks

My Favorite Things

Use the motifs from the six-block quilt *My Favorite Things* which range from Robyn's stylized folk art heart to the more challenging bee skep to practice the art of needleturn appliqué.

By working one block at a time, after the appliqué pieces are cut and applied to the background square you can take it almost anywhere to practice the needleturn technique. After completing the six blocks you'll have mastered many of the challenges of needleturn appliqué and be ready to move on to the practice projects.

Supplies

for finishing MY FAVORITE THINGS

WORK THE BLOCKS IN THE ORDER GIVEN. YOU WILL DEVELOP THE NECESSARY SKILLS AS EACH BLOCK BECOMES MORE CHALLENGING. REFER TO CHAPTER 1 FOR THE SPECIFIC TECHNIQUES FOR LEARNING NEEDLETURN APPLIQUÉ.

Background Fabric for appliqué blocks . . . . .1 yard

Pink Calico Fabric for framing on appliqué blocks . . . .1 yard

Blue Floral Fabric for sashing and corners . . . . .1¾ yards

Green Stripe for border #1 . . . . .½ yard

Rose Floral for outside border and binding . . . . . . .2¼ yards

Backing Fabric seamed to fit a 59" x 77" back . . . . .4½ yards

Cotton batting . . . . .59" x 77" piece

Assorted scraps of fabric for appliqué in a variety of colors.

Threads to match appliqué.

Embroidery floss in several colors to detail appliqué where shown.

The Blocks

My Favorite Things

BEGIN BY CUTTING BACKGROUND SQUARES FOR APPLIQUÉ:

1. Cut 6–14" squares. (The blocks are oversized to allow for trimming later.) Position the appliqué design in the center of the block.

2. For each block, follow the step-by-step instructions on the following pages.

Block 1
for My Favorite Things

Block 1
for MY FAVORITE THINGS

Trace pattern using your preferred method of needleturn appliqué from Chapter 1. Choose desired fabrics. Work in order given below:

1. Center large heart, appliqué.
2. Place small heart, appliqué.

Block 2
for My Favorite Things

Block 2
for MY FAVORITE THINGS

Trace pattern using your preferred method of needleturn appliqué from Chapter 1. Choose desired fabrics. Work in order given below:

1. Center moon, appliqué paying close attention to points on moon.

2. Place stars, appliqué, paying close attention to points on stars.

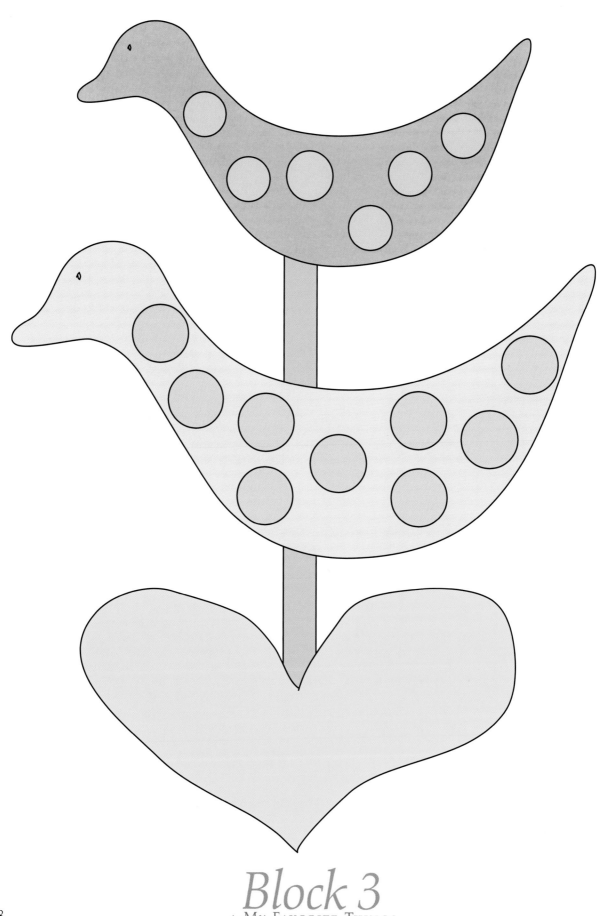

for MY FAVORITE THINGS

Block 3
for MY FAVORITE THINGS

*Trace pattern using your preferred method of needleturn appliqué from Chapter 1.
Choose desired fabrics. Work in order given below:*

1. Lay out design in center of block. Lay out post, appliqué in place.

2. Place heart at bottom of post, appliqué.

3. Place birds on post, appliqué.

4. Place dots on birds, appliqué.

5. Make French knot for eye on each bird using floss. (See Glossary page 78).

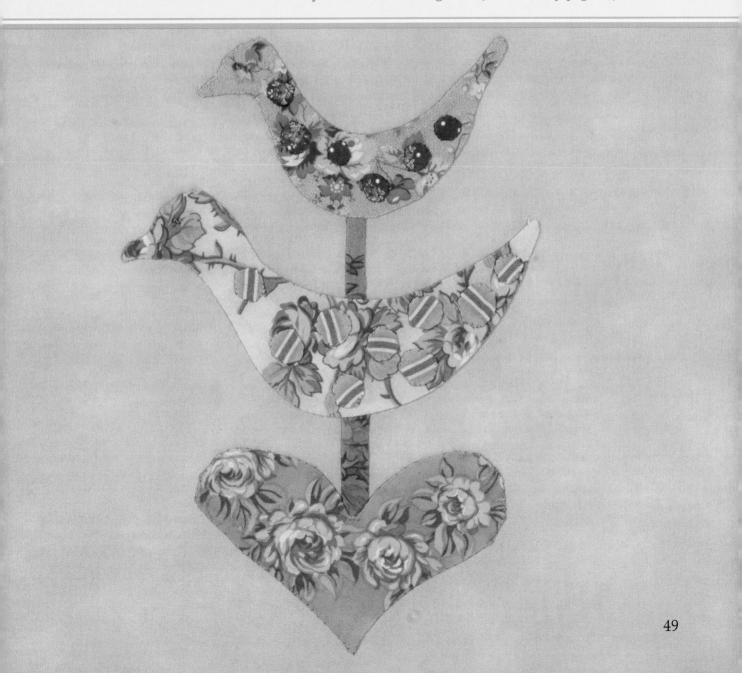

Block 4

for My Favorite Things

Block 4
for My Favorite Things

*Trace pattern using your preferred method of needleturn appliqué from Chapter 1.
Choose desired fabrics. Work in order given below:*

1. Lay out pieces in center of block.
2. Appliqué tail, ears and stem.
3. Lay cat body over stem, tail, and ears; appliqué in place.
4. Appliqué stripes on sides of cat, petals of flower.
5. Appliqué leaves, center of flower, and butterfly.
6. Satin stitch body of butterfly and nose of cat, make French knot for eye, stem stitch antennae and use straight running stitches for whiskers (See Glossary page 78).

Block 5
for My Favorite Things

Block 5
for MY FAVORITE THINGS

Trace pattern using your preferred method of needleturn appliqué from Chapter 1. Choose desired fabrics. Work in order given below:

1. Lay out pieces in center of block.
2. Appliqué stem.
3. Appliqué leaves. Center of each leaf is reverse appliqué technique (page 31).
4. Appliqué large petal piece of flower.
5. Appliqué large circle, medium circle, pointed center, center circle, and small circle center.
6. Appliqué circles around flowers.

Block 6
for My Favorite Things

Block 6
for MY FAVORITE THINGS

Trace pattern using your preferred method of needleturn appliqué from Chapter 1. Choose desired fabrics. Work in order given below:

1. Lay out pieces in center of block.
2. Appliqué star stem, star.
3. Appliqué skep (cover for bee hive).
4. Make bias strip using bias bar technique (page 35). Appliqué in place.
5. Appliqué door, leaves and flowers, overlapping as shown.
6. Appliqué flower centers, bee wings, and bee bodies.
7. Add straight running stitches for bee paths (See Glossary page 78).

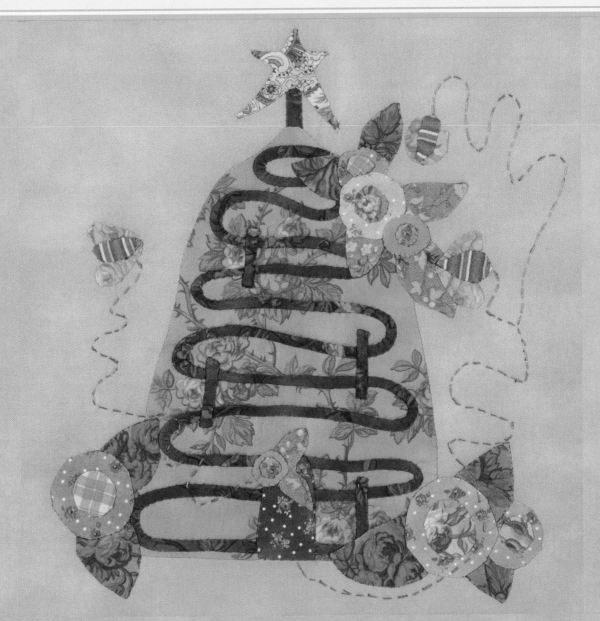

1. Trim appliqué blocks to 12½" square as shown:

2. For block framing cut 10–2½"x 44" strips of pink calico.

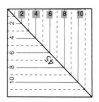 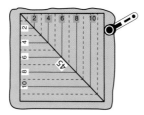

Cut 12–2½"x 12½" rectangles. Sew to top and bottom of the trimmed blocks.
Cut 12–2½"x 16½" rectangles. Sew to the sides of the trimmed blocks. Blocks will now measure 16½" to each unfinished edge.

 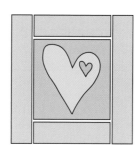

3. For sashing cut 6–2½"x 1¾ yard lengthwise. strips of blue floral.
Cut 3– 2½"x 16½" rectangles from the blue floral. Sew strips between blocks for 3 rows.

Cut 4– 2½"x 34½" strips from the blue floral. Sew strips between rows, to top and bottom. Sew rows together.

The Quilt

4. Cut 2– 2½"x 56½" strips. Sew to sides of piece.

The Quilt

Approximate finished quilt size: 53"x 71"

5. For first border, cut 5– 2"x 44" strips of green stripe. Trim off selvage and seam as needed. Cut 2– 2"x 38½" strips. Sew to top and bottom of piece.

6. For second border, cut 2–2" x 56 ½" strips of green stripe and 4–2" squares of blue floral. Sew the squares to the end of the green stripe strips. Sew to sides of the piece.

7. For outside border, cut 20" off the pink floral and save for the binding. Cut 2– 6½"x 41½" strips, lengthwise. Sew to top and bottom of piece. Cut 2– 6½"x 59½" strips lengthwise and 4–6½" squares of blue floral. Sew the squares to the end of the pink floral strips. Sew to sides of the piece.

8. Baste quilt top with batting and backing. Quilt as desired.

9. Bind quilt using 7–2 ½" strips of the pink floral (border fabric).

1. Piece the binding strips on the diagonal.

2. Fold the strip in half lengthwise, wrong sides together, and press.

3. Unfold and trim one end at a 45° angle. Turn under the edge ¼" and press. Refold the strip.

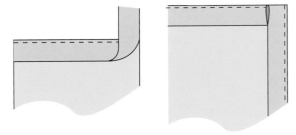

4. With raw edges of the binding and quilt even, stitch with a ⅜" seam allowance, starting 2" from the angled end.

5. Miter the binding at the corners. As you approach a corner of the quilt, stop sewing ⅜" from the corner of the quilt.

6. Clip the threads and remove the quilt from under the presser foot.

7. Flip the binding strip up and away from the quilt, then fold the binding down even with the raw edge of the quilt. Begin sewing at the upper edge. Miter all 4 corners in this manner.

8. Trim the end of the binding so it can be tucked inside of the beginning binding about ⅜". Finish stitching the seam.

9. Turn the folded edge of the binding over the raw edges and to the back of the quilt so that the stitching line does not show. Hand-sew the binding in place, folding in the mitered corners as you stitch.

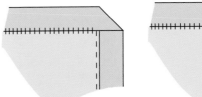
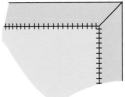

60

The Practice Pieces

for NEEDLETURN APPLIQUÉ

Master the art of needleturn appliqué using practice pieces that complement the six-block quilt for a glorious bed, bath or gift collection inspired by Robyn Pandolph's enduring folk art designs.

Choose from an array of pillows, fingertip towels, linens, framed pictures, boxes, a diary cover and more. Fabrics for the duvet cover and other bedding accessories are from Robyn's *Sentimental Journey* collection designed for South Sea Imports®, available at most independent quilt shops.

Practice Pieces
FOR NEEDLETURN APPLIQUÉ

FINGERTIP TOWELS

Materials:

 Yellow floral scraps

Blue floral scraps

Yellow silk ribbon

Blue silk ribbon

Linen fingertip towels

Instructions:

1. Using the small heart design from Block 1 (page 44), or a heart of your size and choice, appliqué using your preferred method of needleturn appliqué.

2. Appliqué in center of fingertip towel using matching thread.

3. Make two lazy daisy stitches next to each heart using silk ribbon (See Glossary, page 78).

LINEN NAPKIN

Materials:

Linen napkin

Scraps for appliqué

Silk ribbon, if desired

Instructions:

1. Increase or decrease desired appliqué designs on copier.

2. Appliqué using preferred method of appliqué. Insert silk ribbon along edge of napkin, weaving it in and out, if desired.

Practice Pieces
FOR NEEDLETURN APPLIQUÉ

Practice Pieces
FOR NEEDLETURN APPLIQUÉ

HEART-SHAPED PILLOW

Materials:

Heart-shaped pillow form

> *(approximately 16" x 14" or cut a heart pattern from freezer paper and stuff pillow with fiberfill)*

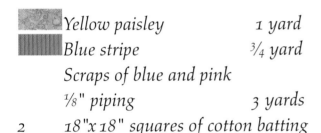

Yellow paisley	*1 yard*
Blue stripe	*¾ yard*
Scraps of blue and pink	
⅛" piping	*3 yards*
2 *18"x18" squares of cotton batting*	

Instructions:

1. Using manufacturer's pattern piece or your own, cut out front and back of pillow from yellow paisley.

2. Layer with cotton batting and mark grid lines approximately 2" apart. Machine quilt.

3. Appliqué heart designs from Block 1 (page 44) using your preferred method of needleturn appliqué.

4. Make Piping:
   a. Cut 1½" bias strips from blue stripe as described in bias bar appliqué (page 34).

Measure heart shape for exact length and seam strips as needed. (Approximately 3 yards).

b. Using sewing machine and zipper foot insert piping into fold of bias strips, as shown:

c. Baste with machine to right side of front and back of pillow using zipper foot.

5. Make Ruffle:
   a. Cut 4 – 4" x 44" strips of yellow paisley.
   b. Seam two strips to measure 75" each.
   c. Sew into a loop.
   d. Press in half horizontally right side out.
   e. Stitch two rows of basting stitches for gathering at ¼" and ½" from raw edge.
   f. Pull up threads and gather easing and pinning around the top and back of pillow, on top of piping.
   g. Machine baste in place using zipper foot.

6. Cut 2 – 4" x 44" strips of blue stripe fabric. Seam together to measure approximately 48" or the measurement around the outside of the heart pattern.

7. Pin top to side bands. Sew.

8. Pin back to side bands. Sew, leaving an opening for turning and to stuff or insert pillow form.

9. Whip stitch closed.

Practice Pieces
FOR NEEDLETURN APPLIQUÉ

JOURNAL COVER

Materials:

1   *Journal*
        (approximately 8½"x 11"x ¾")
Pink floral   *1 yard*
    Scraps for moon and star
    Thin craft batting
       22"x 13" rectangle
    ⅜" deckle edge ribbon
    ⅛" piping   *2 yards*
Embroidery floss
(NOTE: adjust to size of your journal)

Instructions:

1. Cut 1– 13"x 22" rectangle of pink floral.

2. Layer with craft batting and grid quilt, approximately 1" apart.

3. Appliqué moon and one star design from Block 2 (page 46) to front side of cover using your preferred method of needleturn appliqué.

4. Trim cover to 11½"x 19½". Adjust to size if necessary.

5. Make piping according to directions for Heart-Shaped Pillow (page 65), using pink floral.

6. Machine stitch, using zipper foot, piping all around outside edge of cover.

7. Cut 2– 7"x 11½" rectangles of pink floral for side flaps. Make a 1" hem on one 11½" side of each rectangle.
Cut 1–11½"x 19½" rectangle of pink floral for lining. Machine baste side flaps to end of lining, right sides up, as shown.

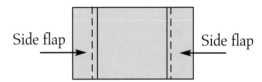

Side flap →   ← Side flap

8. Layer and pin journal front and lining right sides together. Insert 12" of ribbon on each side. Machine sew with a zipper foot, leaving an opening for turning.

9. Clip corners, turn. Whip stitch opening closed.

10. Insert journal.

11. Tie ribbon in a bow.

Practice Pieces
FOR NEEDLETURN APPLIQUÉ

Embellished Pillow Case

Materials:

Purchased Pillow Case

Yellow floral   ⅔ yard

Green plaid   ½ yard

Scraps for appliqué

Embroidery floss

Note: If you choose to make a pair,
adjust your materials accordingly.

Instructions:

1. Cut 2– 10"x 44" strips of yellow floral fabric.

2. Seam at both 10" ends, forming a loop.

3. Press in half horizontally. (wrong sides together).

4. Sew basting stitches for gathering at ¼" and ½" from raw edge.

5. Pull up threads and gather to fit at the cuff of pillowcase.

6. Baste down raw edge.

7. Cut 2" bias strips from green plaid as described in bias bar appliqué (page 34). Seam as needed. You will need approximately 44".

8. Press a ½" seam allowance along one long edge.

9. Lay right side to top of ruffle aligning raw edges. Machine stitch through all.

10. Press and fold bias over raw edges and top stitch folded edge down.

11. Appliqué the following using your preferred method of needleturn appliqué:

Butterfly from Block 4, increased to desired size on copier.

Bee and flowers from Block 6, increased to desired size on copier.

Practice Pieces
FOR NEEDLETURN APPLIQUÉ

RECTANGULAR PILLOW

Materials:

1   18"x 32" pillow form
       (or size of your choice)

Yellow stripe   ⅓ yard

Pink floral for ruffle   ⅓ yard

Blue floral
     2– 13"x 19" rectangles

Yellow floral
     2– 4"x 13" rectangles

Green plaid
     1– 19"x 33" for back
     1– 12"x 19" for front center

Purple calico   ½ yard

¼" piping   3 yards

Instructions:

1. Increase Bird Pattern (page 48) to fit center plaid panel.

2. Appliqué using your preferred method of needleturn appliqué.

3. Fold yellow stripe in half horizontally. Press.

4. Insert yellow stripe in seam with blue floral and plaid appliqué, forming front of pillow.

5. Cut 2" bias from purple calico as described in bias bar appliqué (page 34). Seam as needed. You will need approximately 3 yards.

6. Make piping as described in Heart-Shaped Pillow (page 65). Sew to pillow top rounding corners, using a zipper foot.

7. Cut 2– 10"x 44" pink floral strips for ruffle. Seam together at both 10" ends, forming a loop.

8. Press in half horizontally, (wrong sides together).

9. Sew basting stitches for gathering ¼" and ½" from raw edge.

10. Gather to fit pillow top. Pinning through piping, machine baste using a zipper foot.

11. Pin pillow back and pillow front right sides together. Machine sew through all using the basting stitches as a guide. Leave an opening for turning.

12. Turn right side out. Insert pillow form. Whip stitch opening closed.

Practice Pieces
FOR NEEDLETURN APPLIQUÉ

Framed Blocks

Materials:

*Purchased or recycled picture
frames, no glass is required
Miscellaneous scraps for
background and appliqué
Scraps of thin craft batting*

Instructions:

1. Cut background piece using the cardboard
insert as a pattern.

2. Appliqué using your preferred method of
needleturn appliqué your choice of patterns,
increasing or decreasing in size to fit nicely in
your frame.

3. Sew borders or make a flat fold of fabric
at edges.

4. Layer batting, cardboard back and appliqué
piece, gluing if needed.

5. Insert in frame.

Practice Pieces
FOR NEEDLETURN APPLIQUÉ

ROUND NESTING BOXES

Materials:

>*Set of stacking round craft boxes*
>>*(approximate diameters of 3", 4" and 5")*
>*Miscellaneous scraps to fit around boxes*
>>*and for appliqué*
>*Scraps of thin craft batting*
>*Scraps of lace and ribbon for trimming*
>*Tacky craft glue or craft spray adhesive*

Instructions:

1. To cover box, measure and cut fabric 1" taller and 1" larger than circumference of box. Cut rectangle this size.

2. Attach to box using craft glue or craft spay adhesive. Clip at bottom and fold over, glue. Roll top edge to inside of box, glue.

3. Cut a circle of craft batting the size of top. Cut a circle of fabric approximately 1" larger.

4. Grid quilt approximately ¾" to craft batting.

5. Choose desired appliqué designs increasing or decreasing in size as needed.

6. Appliqué using preferred method of needleturn appliqué.

7. Clip edges and glue to top of box.

8. Cover sides with ribbons and trims, as desired.

Practice Pieces
FOR NEEDLETURN APPLIQUÉ

TALL BOX

Materials:

1 Tall craft cardboard box
   (approximately 5"x 5"x 14")
Blue stripe fabric
   22"x16" piece
Thin craft batting
   22"x 16" piece
Pink calico
   10" square
Thin craft Batting
   5" square
Scraps for cat pattern (page 50)
Embroidery floss
Tacky glue or
   Spray craft adhesive

Instructions:

1. Appliqué cat to center of blue stripe fabric using your preferred method of needleturn appliqué. Align as desired on your box for proper placement. Follow appliqué instructions (page 50).

2. Quilt around cat to craft batting.

3. Machine baste all edges. Rotary pink one 16" side for overlap.

4. Starting at front, glue cat piece to box, following manufacturer's instructions.

5. Fold excess fabric around to inside. Glue in place.

6. Fold over bottom. Miter corners. Secure with glue.

7. For the lid, glue 5" square of batting to top of lid. Using pink calico fold and glue around lid mitering corners. Trim as needed.

Practice Pieces
FOR NEEDLETURN APPLIQUÉ

Glossary
UNDERSTAND THE TERMS

Appliqué: Fabric shapes or motifs that are sewn to another fabric for extra dimension or interest.

Background Fabric: The fabric to which the appliqué pieces are sewn.

Backing: Fabric for the back lining of the quilt.

Batting: A thin soft cotton layer that is between the backing and front of quilt.

Bias: The diagonal of the fabric weave. It stretches.

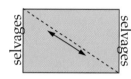

Bias Press Bars: Nylon or metal bars used to help with pressing of bias strips.

Binding: Strips of fabric that are sewn over the trimmed raw edges of the finished quilt.

Border: A frame of fabric around the joined blocks of a quilt.

Freezer Paper: Paper that has a dull paper side and shiny wax or plastic side. Available at grocery stores.

Inside Curve: Concave curve.

Lengthwise Grain of Fabric: When the grain or long edge of fabric runs parallel to the selvage.

Milliner's Needles: Long thin needle used for hand appliqué and sewing.

Needleturn Appliqué: A technique of hand appliqué where the needle is used as a tool to turn the seam allowance under the appliqué before stitching down to the background with small stitches.

Outside Curve: Convex curve.

Reverse Appliqué: Designs made by cutting out a shape in the top appliqué and exposing the fabric underneath. The edges of the shape are turned under and the edges stitched.

Rotary Cutter, Mat and Ruler: Allows for easily cutting straight shapes. Available at quilt shops and sewing stores.

Sashing: Strips of fabric that are sewn between quilt blocks as a way to join the blocks into a top.

Seam Allowance: The distance between the cut and sewn edge of patchwork or appliqué.

Sharps: Small thin needles used for hand appliqué and sewing.

Sandpaper or Sandpaper Board: Helps with the tracing the appliqué shapes onto fabric. Available at hardware and sewing stores.

Scissors:
Fabric Scissors; good sharp scissors for cutting fabric shapes and trimming threads.

Paper Scissors: Good scissors that won't be hurt by cutting paper or template plastic.

Straw Needles: Long flexible needle used for hand appliqué and sewing.

Strip: A width of fabric cut from fabric. Sometimes it will be a specific length.

Template Plastic: A sturdy but thin plastic used for template making. Available at quilt shops and sewing stores.

Thimble: A protective cover worn on the finger to protect it from the needle when pushing through fabric.

Embroidery Stitches

French Knot Stitch

1. Bring the needle and floss up at A. Pull the floss taut with your left hand. Wrap the floss around the needle once. More wraps will make a larger knot.
2. Insert the needle at B and pull the floss so the knot is pushed close to the fabric. Keep the tension even, but do not pull too tightly or you will be unable to pull the needle through the knot and fabric.
3. Pull the floss down at B. Keep holding the floss taut until most of the floss has been pulled through.

Lazy Daisy Stitch

1. Bring the floss up at A. Hold the floss against the fabric with your thumb while forming the loop. Insert

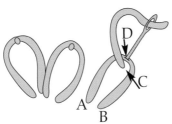

the needle through the fabric at B and bring the needle up at C in the same stitch. Pull the floss through, keeping the loop full and puffy. Pierce the top edge of the loop at D and pull through. This will secure the lazy daisy from shifting.

Satin Stitch

1. Bring the needle up at A, then down at B. This completes one stitch. Keep the floss flat, making sure that each stitch is close to, but not overlapping, the previous stitch. The distance for A to B is variable for each stitch, depending on the space or the area to be covered.

Straight Running Stitch

1. This is a simple, flat stitch from A to B. Its length is variable, depending upon the appearance and desired results.

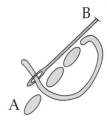

Stem Stitch

1. Begin the stitch by bringing your needle up at A. Hold the floss flat on the fabric with your thumb to either side of the stem line.
2. The stitch from B to A is a single stem stitch. This is repeated as many times as is needed for the length of the stem.